For Rashmi

Contents

-5-

Famagusta

(Shortlisted for the Sultan Padamsee
Playwriting Award, 2020)

This one-act play is set in the living room of the Siddiquis in Lahore *circa* 2000, when they have a visitor - a retired Colonel from India. A new friendship flourishes that evening with shared experiences at Partition and in the army. But as the night progresses, a deeper reason is revealed to actually bring them together – one that could threaten their newfound friendship forever.

Famagusta was first staged at the Dara Shukoh Library, Partition Museum, New Delhi on 17 & 18 May, 2025 with the following cast:

Fatima Siddiqui: Divya Yadav
Brig. Junaid Siddiqui: Neel Madhav Gupta:
Col. P.N. Jaswal: Chinmaya Sharma

Director: Vikramjeet Sinha
(Artists' Amateur Guild)

Famagusta

(A Play in One Act)

Cast (in order)

Fatima Siddiqui *f*, mid 60s, Pakistani
Brig. Junaid Siddiqui *m*, late 60s, her husband
Col. P.N. Jaswal *m*, early 70s, Indian

Scene 1

Stage black. A screen in the background streams rapidly changing sepia photographs from the Partition – of people milling near (and on) trains, of them walking in the thousands, of violence and death. Then, a few shots of Lahore – its masjids, mandis and maidans. The screen flickers to a stop with a blurred photograph of what looks like a medallion shaped as a square cross.

Scene 2

Lahore. Circa 2000. Late evening. The living room of the Siddiquis. Comfortable sofas, teakwood coffee table, floor lamps, a book on the side table with an ash-tray and a pipe, a well-stocked bar, Cashmere rug on the floor. Ornate brass candle-stands arranged on the cabinet. A portrait of the Brigadier in his military uniform with medals hangs on the wall, bearing a brass inscription that is illegible. Book-shelf with a mix of books on travel, Urdu poetry, Sufi literature, military history, and others...

Brig. Siddiqui *clean-shaven, balding, polished, is dressed in a linen shirt, comfortable trousers and Moccasins.* **Fatima** *feisty, slightly grey, wears a traditional salwar-kameez and a chunky silver pendant. The LP plays 'Nit Khair Mangan'.*

Fatima Is your drink alright?

Brig. Siddiqui Just perfect Poochie.

Fatima Don't call me that!

Brig. Siddiqui You know, when your father approved our alliance, he said 'Always take care of my Poochie'. So, it's a promise I made to him.

Fatima You seem to have kept half your promise then.

Brig Siddiqui Ha! The important half.

Fatima Remember, a promise to a General is sacrosanct.

Brig. Siddiqui What about a dead General?

Fatima *(Sighs in exasperation)* He watches over us, beware. (*Beat*) But Junaid, is this a wise decision?

Brig. Siddiqui What is?

Fatima You know… Inviting the Indian officer over for a drink.

Brig. Siddiqui Never made a wiser decision in my life.

Fatima You better know what you're doing. I've known you to be a lot of things, and wise isn't one of them.

He looks at her blankly.

Fatima You do know this is sensitive. Delicate. Dangerous even.

Brig. Siddiqui (*Beneath his breath*) It's alright…

Fatima What did you say?

Brig. Siddiqui It's al-right, I said.

Fatima: (*Moves stage centre, agitated. Speaks to the audience, but looking into space, while **Brig. Siddiqui** lights a pipe and smokes it slowly in the background*) 'It's alright', he says. It's not alright! This is an *Indian* officer being invited to our home, the home of a Pakistani officer, the home of a Pakistani officer's daughter. It makes me nervous to the pit of my stomach. Junaid doesn't think it's just another drink with a mate, does he? And remember, things between us... between our countries are never normal. Our history is complicated and violent. People do have affection for one another, but there's also so much hatred. And worse still, so much scope for misunderstanding. Doesn't Junaid see this! Or does he not care. I know he has his reasons, but still... he knows what happened with Nadeem. *(More directly to the audience)* Nadeem is my brother – Captain Nadeem Malik of the 15 Punjab Regiment. *(Softer, with a tinge of sadness)* Formerly, of the 15 Punjab Regiment. He was such a promising officer, went to the Pakistan Military Academy and was going to go places. Like his father. And then? *(Worked up)* He goes to this national security seminar in Washington, meets an Indian delegate there and falls in love! Yes, I'll grant she's an American citizen, but with a name like Reema and family in India who the hell was going to understand! We begged him to forget her, but no. Ziddi hai! He says 'I'll marry her and no one else.' Next thing you know, he informs his Commanding Officer, who, obviously, goes by the rules and says 'Son, it's her or the army'. It's her, obviously. And Nadeem puts in his papers, moves to the US and now does some small-time real estate work in Minneapolis. But he drinks big I hear. Reema tells me on the sly. Obviously, he would! I know how much he loved being in the army. Abba stopped talking to him soon after. Can I blame him? At dinners, his colleagues would taunt him at earshot 'Janab Hindustani bahu laaye hain!'. I can never forget the shame… the pain on Abba's face. For a proud Pakistani General to have to listen to such ridicule is worse than death. He just became a recluse after Nadeem's episode. (*Pause*) And now Junaid goes and invites an Indian officer home (*Sighs*) Allah hifazat kare… (*Moves back to the scene*)

(*To* **Brig. Siddiqui**, *almost pleading*) You do know this is sensitive. Delicate. Dangerous even.

Brig. Siddiqui (*Stoically*) It's alright.

Fatima (*Resigned*) Well, I dearly hope so. (*Beat. Now upbeat, with resolve*) Let me go fix some pakodas and kheer for our guest then. We need to show him what real Punjabi hospitality is.

Fatima exits. **Brig. Siddiqui** *drifts towards the LP player, turns up the volume and stands by the window, gazing outwards. Then looks at his watch.*

Brig. Siddiqui It's almost 8. (*To Fatima, across the room*) Your 'real Punjabi hospitality' better be ready soon. The Colonel should be arriving. These Indian officers are bloody punctual, though never a minute early. Something they're said to have imbibed from Field Marshal Cariappa. Unlike our chaps, who show up half an hour early, especially when tipple is on offer.

Fatima Oh please! Don't malign our officers just like that. They're among the finest in the world, I hear.

Brig. Siddiqui Is that from forty years ago? Drilled into your pretty head by your old man.

Fatima Why does *he* get dragged into everything! And remember, he did win the Sitara-e-Jurat.

Brig. Siddiqui Well, I won the Tamgha-e-Jurat – that hasn't helped you see me any differently. Besides, your father won it... gratuitously.

Fatima Gra-tu-it-ous-ly. What the hell do you mean!

Brig. Siddiqui You know what I mean, When the war broke out...

Mid-sentence, the doorbell rings. **Brig. Siddiqui** *turns down the music and moves briskly to the door to open it. At the steps, is* **Col. Jaswal.** *A grey, unyielding man, who looks fit beyond his years. He wears a crisp shirt, trousers, well-polished shoes and a cravat. Pointed moustache, military style.*

Brig. Siddiqui Good evening Sir! Welcome to our home.

Col. Jaswal Good evening Brigadier. A rare honour to be with you.

Brig. Siddiqui *(Loudly, to Fatima)* Fatima, our guest is here! Won't you come say hello.

Fatima enters. Salaam, Bhaijaan! Welcome...

Col. Jaswal *(Formally)* Thank you Ma'am. A pleasure to meet you.

Brig. Siddiqui Come Colonel, do make yourself comfortable. What would you like to drink?

Col. Jaswal *(Peering at the bottles on the bar)* I'll have a whiskey-soda please.

Brig. Siddiqui Ice?

Col. Jaswal Three cubes, thank you.

Brig. Siddiqui That's as many as I like them! *(In an officer-like voice)* Two cubes, too bold. Four cubes, too cold! (**Col. Jaswal** *laughs along, politely. Drinks are fixed)* Cheers, Sir!

Col. Jaswal Cheers. To our countries.

Brig. Siddiqui To our friendship. *(To Fatima)* Won't you join us for a drink?

Fatima Once I bring those pakodas out for the both of you. Will then let you fix me some Chardonnay. *(As she exits, she sings the first two lines of Asha Bhonsle's song Chain Se Humko Kabhi… to her husband with a look of mischief. Col Jaswal laughs in fulsome delight.)*

Brig. Siddiqui *(Settling into his favourite chair)* So Sir, how has Lahore treated you thus far?

Col. Jaswal Like I'm one of her own, I must say. Warmth, good food and colour everywhere I go.

Brig. Siddiqui In true Punjabi style Sir, if I may say so myself.

Fatima *(Returning from the kitchen with a plate)* As they say, 'Jis Lahore nahin vekhiya, o jamiya nahin.'*

Col. Jaswal Indeed, Ma'am. I now feel a sense of completion having finally visited Lahore. This is where my wife's parents were from. I must thank you Brigadier for making this possible. Those letters you wrote to the Army Headquarters in Delhi greatly helped in arranging my trip here.

Brig. Siddiqui Not at all Sir. The least I could do for a fellow cavalry officer. Would never do it for the poor bloody infantry!

They laugh, with a regimental esprit de corps.

Col. Jaswal The armoured corps is truly the pride of any fauj. My son Lieutenant Mohit was a cavalry officer himself. (***Fatima*** *abruptly exits as* **Brig. Siddiqui** *looks edgily into his glass. Awkward pause where neither speaks.)* As much as I've welcomed your gesture Brigadier, I do wonder what prompted you to single me out. It is... *(searching for the right word)* unusual, shall we say.

Brig. Siddiqui *(Shiftily)* Well, Sir... ahem... I had read about your exploits in combat, and that, like myself... in

---

* One who hasn't seen Lahore, is yet to be born

fact, like both Fatima and myself… you are a Partition migrant too. I thought it would be apt to try and facilitate your visit to Pakistan to make it to your birthplace, something we have long wanted to do ourselves but could not… together that is… I did manage to visit Delhi on a symposium in 1993… chanced upon the spot where our family home stood. You won't believe what it is now… a part of the damn Pandara Road Market! I have to say the food there is quite amazing though… The rogan josh, kya baat hai! Almost as good as the stuff you get here…

Col. Jaswal (*noticing the Brigadier veering off into a ramble*) Well, that makes perfect sense then. Your writing to me. Or rather writing *for* me to the Army HQ. Thank you again… I'm truly obliged.

Brig. Siddiqui (*Now a little more assured*) Very welcome Sir. Inshallah, you will enjoy your visit to Quetta over the coming days. It is a long journey I must warn you.

Col. Jaswal Yes, I'm aware of that… a full day on the road. But rather picturesque.

Brig. Siddiqui Oh yes! Once you start nearing the hills it's absolute magic. Jannat…

Fatima now joins them with some kheer and a bowl of dry fruit. **Brig. Siddiqui** *gets up to go to the bar and pour her a glass of wine.*

Fatima You will love Quetta, Bhaijaan. My Abba was at the Staff College there for a course when I was about sixteen and I still have wonderful memories of the place...

Col. Jaswal Fatima-ji, it is fifty-three years ago that we left Quetta and I still remember it like it was yesterday...

Fatima Do tell us about it... if you wouldn't mind that is. *(To **Brig. Sidiqqui** who returns with her drink)* Shukriya, ji.

Col. Jaswal Where do I begin! Dad was posted at Quetta. He was not an officer, but a 'civvie'. The catering manager at the Mess, which was perhaps the most stressful job to have at the College. British officers were extremely particular about their food, and more particular about their breakfast, which followed the chhota hazari and PT at dawn. Every day, a set menu. If I remember correctly, fried eggs and bacon on Mondays *(Thinking)*... porridge and boiled eggs Tuesdays, and so through the week. Dad in fact converted them to poori-aaloo, which they took to rather well. That became staple on Fridays....

(The couple laughs.)

Mum was expecting me in 1927 and I believe I was taken to her native village in Khanewal for delivery. A good ten hours by bus... one bloody bumpy ride it used to be as I remember it the few times I made that trek later. So technically, my birthplace is Khanewal, though my passport says Quetta. But all my memories are of Quetta... I hope I'm not boring you?

Brig. Siddiqui Not at all Sir, carry on! *He takes the glass from* **Col. Jaswal** *to refill their drinks, smiling at Fatima who is taking in the moment.)*

Col. Jaswal *(Continues)* Life seemed secure there. It never felt like the Brits would ever leave, though one often heard of Gandhi's growing resistance of the Empire. Funnily, Jinnah was never taken seriously in these parts at the time. Dad had plans to groom me for the Fauj after college, obviously influenced by the dapper Tommies who were posted there for their staff courses. I was in the second year of my B.A. when, all of a sudden in August 1947 it was announced that some sort of a partition would be worked out and we would have to leave for *(makes double quotations with his fingers)* "India". I said to Dad, 'what do you mean, leave for India – this *is* India!' He was baffled too, but tried explaining that India would now be divided into two and where we were, was not where we belonged. *(Pausing to sip his drink)* Some said this was temporary and we'd return in a few months. Others spoke of brutal violence that had begun to break out at the borders. We were, of course.... worried... where would we go? Would we be safe? What of our home and belongings? What if we were assaulted, killed even?

(They nod, with rapt attention.)

Sensing our fears, Lieutenant Colonel Burgess a deputy commandant at the College - God bless his soul – figured a solution for us. The perks of being a loyal part of the Staff College perhaps. He arranged for a Dakota to fly us across to Delhi. My parents, brother Baldev, three sisters and I got on that nineteen-seater with a young officer, and were flown across to safety. Never did I imagine that would be the last time I'd see Quetta – its wild, icy mountains and its pristine emptiness. Landing in Delhi took me on a long, unknown course – Shimla, the Army, etc. that I don't want to bore you with. I must say, we were much luckier than the others who succumbed in transit. And at the same time, the old bonds remained. The caretaker of my mother's house in Khanewal, Rahim Chacha, continued to look after the house for – you may not believe this – over ten years after we left! *(The Siddiquis look at each other in amazement)* He wrote to us, praying we would return. Of course, we did not. Could not. And he died protecting our home, still hoping we would return. For every story of usurpation of land and property, there are such unsung accounts that exist too...

Silence.

Brig. Siddiqui This is a truly amazing account, Sir. I had wanted to share our experience at Partition too, but now, I just want to savour your version. It has touched me deeply.

Fatima That makes the two of us, Bhaijaan. Such quirks of fate... such unnecessary trauma and pain. For what? Are we better off with this? I don't know. It's not something one can say openly, especially as an army officer's wife, but what has to be said, has to be said. What have we *truly* gained by our separation? Are our countries more prosperous, more powerful? Are we, as people, better off? I always wonder at the senselessness of the violence and the loss. Munir Niazi's nazm ends with these lines that have always summed up Partition for me – 'Kuch shaher de log vi zaalam saan, kuch menoo maran da shoq vi si'.[†]

Brig. Siddiqui *(Trying to lighten up things, jovially)* What if we were indeed never partitioned Colonel, then what?

Col. Jaswal Well, for starters, Javed Miandad would never have played test cricket!

They laugh, almost in respite.

Brig. Siddiqui Come on Sir! Our bowling side would have almost entirely been from these parts. Imran, Akram, Waqar, Qadir... And our umpires would have won us every game against the rest of the world!

Col. Jaswal Now that part I fully endorse! Fully. Endorse.

[†]   The folks in the city were indeed cruel, but I too was fond of dying.

More laughter.

Brig. Siddiqui Let me tell you an India – Pakistan joke...

Col. Jaswal Be my guest.

Brig. Siddiqui An Indian and a Pakistani found themselves seated next to each other on a flight...

Fatima Oh, Junaid, not the same one again!

Brig. Siddiqui *(Undeterred)* At some point, the Pakistani who is seated at the aisle, gets up to go get some water from the counter at the back of the aircraft. He asks his Indian neighbour if he would like some water too, and he says 'yes please, thank you.' As the Pakistani is out of sight, the Indian notices the Pakistani's shoes on the floor next to him. He promptly picks one up and spits in it. *(The two men laugh. **Fatima** seems unimpressed)* Soon, the Pakistani returns, and offers a glass of water to the Indian who gulps it down gleefully. The Pakistani then turns to his co-passenger and says, 'Janab, how long is this going to go on? Spitting in each other's shoes... spitting in each other's water.'

They all laugh heartily.

Brig. Siddiqui *(To Fatima)* See Begum? It's still funny no matter how many times you repeat it.

Fatima *waves him off.*

Col. Jaswal I have a joke of my own. A real life one, in fact. Fatima-ji I hope you will forgive the slightly naughty content.

Fatima Bhaijaan, in this household nothing is out of bounds, so please don't pull your punches.

Col. Jaswal Excellent! So this was told to me by a retired Air Commodore, who was the Air Attaché at Islamabad sometime in the late '80s. Once, he was on a visit to the air force station at Sargodha and was taking a look at the newly acquired F-16s imported by the Pakistan Air Force from America. As he stood admiring one of those jets, a young, strapping Punjabi wing-commander came up to him and said mockingly 'Janab, tussi kaddi aisa jahaz vekhiya vi hai?'.[‡] The Air Commodore, Punjabi himself, looked the wing-commander straight in the eye and replied 'Puttar, main te teri ma da yaar aan.'[§]

They laugh uproariously. Nina Simone plays in a lively jazz-foxtrot version, that fills the room and slowly drowns the lines that follow.

Brig. Siddiqui *(Still laughing)* Enough to start a war that exchange! I hope they were soon separated.

Col. Jaswal Separated!? Apparently a bottle of Black Label was opened later that evening, which the two gentlemen polished off effortlessly.

---

‡ Mister, have you even seen such a jet?
§ Son, I am your mother's lover.

Brig. Siddiqui Kya baat hai! *(They laugh)*

Col. Jaswal *(To Brig Siddiqui)* May I use your restroom please?

Brig. Siddiqui Certainly Sir *(Gets up to escort him to the bedroom, and returns to find Fatima standing near the door, glaring)*

Fatima *(In a hushed but agitated tone)* You'll need to talk to him about what you wanted to soon. This is getting very uncomfortable!

Brig. Siddiqui Yes, yes...

Fatima Then do so as soon as he returns!

Brig. Siddiqui Alright. And please keep it down, these officers have ears like hares!

Fatima Junaid, even now think about it. He seems like a good soul and let's leave things as they are...

Col. Jaswal *(Off stage, whistling a tune, returns and spots a photo frame on the cabinet)* May I ask who this is?

Brig. Siddiqui This is Fatima's father, Gen Malik.

Col. Jaswal *(Picking it up)* Quite a handsome man! Reminds me a little of my father.

Brig. Siddiqui Makes us brothers then Sir.

Fatima gestures in exasperation to Brig. Siddiqui, clearly uncomfortable with how close the two men seem to growing as friends.

Col. Jaswal You can be the younger brother I've never had. *(Puts his arm around Brig. Siddiqui)*

Brig. Siddiqui Cheers Sir

Lights fade with the two men clinking their glasses, and Fatima standing impassively by a chair.

<h1 style="text-align:center">Scene 3</h1>

*The Siddiquis'. About an hour later. **Brig. Siddiqui** stands at the window puffing on his pipe. General sense of joie de vivre, now that they are all more relaxed and have had a drink or two. The men are in an animated conversation, before settling into their chairs.*

Fatima *(Nursing her second glass of wine. To **Col. Jaswal**)* I was reading recently that there is a locality in Karachi called Bangalore Town. So named owing to the large number of Sindhi migrants from Bangalore at Partition. This was news to me. Were you aware of it Bhaijaan?

Col. Jaswal *(More chatty now)* Fatima-ji, you must call me Ponty. As is wont in the army, everyone gets a nickname. Mine was simply a reworking of my initials P. and N. Good old Phool Nath became Ponty. I'm sure your husband has one too. *(**Fatima** looks at **Brig. Siddiqui** and they smile, as if in secret know of something)*

Fatima *(Volunteering)* He was known as Bud. For his fondness of Marlon Brando.

Col. Jaswal Ah, the Godfather himself! *(**Brig. Siddiqui** blushes slightly. To Fatima)* Ummm... you asked me about Bangalore Town... No, I wasn't aware of this. How interesting to learn of it though! Unlike here in Pakistan, the Sindhis in India still have no state of their own. All we have is a few Karachi Bakeries that recognize their native land. As for Bangalore itself, I have to confess I haven't visited it in all my life. Somehow, our postings were all in the North or North-East. It's is a lovely city with friendly people I hear. *(He gulps the remainder of his drink, and looks at his watch)* Folks, I should be off soon. The dining room at the Gymkhana closes at 2230 hrs sharp.

Fatima We really wish you could have stayed for dinner... Ponty.

Col. Jaswal *is amused.*

Brig. Siddiqui One for the road, Sir?

Col. Jaswal Erm... why not. Bud. A small please.

Brig. Siddiqui Coming right up. *(He goes to the bar to fix a round of drinks. As he is pouring drinks, the lights go out.)* Behench#d! *(**Fatima** glares at him)* Man has landed on the moon but this power problem can never be solved!

Col. Jaswal It's the case everywhere!

Fatima *lights the two brass candle-stands, and sits down filling small bowls with the kheer she has prepared. The rest of the play proceeds in candle light.*

Brig. Siddiqui (*Returning with drinks*) Here you are, Sir.

Col. Jaswal Thank you!

Brig. Siddiqui (*Settling uneasily in his chair, takes 2 or 3 large sips of his drink, in slience. The mood begins to change. Tentatively*) Sir, there was something I wanted to tell you before you left. (**Col. Jaswal** *looks at him impassively.*) There was a reason I tried to get in touch with you with those letters...... I mean, a reason other than that I told you earlier... (**Col. Jaswal** *listens, unmoved.* **Brig. Siddiqui** *speaks these lines firmly, but with a certain restraint, regret even*) Sir, as you know, I saw action in 1971 as did you. We were perhaps in different theatres, you in the Eastern one as far as I know and I, in the Western, with the 13 Lancers. We were commissioned to Bara Pind in December to hold the international boundary as best as we could. We were told of the Indian cavalry's advance into our parts and ceding any part of Punjab would have been crucial, as you can understand. (**Col. Jaswal** *sits up in his chair and begins to listen more intently*) For that week or so, both sides were gridlocked with no quarter given. Close to the 16th of December, news began to trickle in that Dhaka would fall to the Indian Army, which was helped by the Mukti Bahini. The separation of East Pakistan seemed inevitable. This felt like a limb being severed without anesthesia... Anyhow, the very serious concern on the West was, what if the Indians overrun the Punjab and enter Lahore? That would have been unthinkable for us... you will understand. News was also trickling in of a renewed tank attack at the border we were protecting. On the morning of the 16th the news was confirmed. Indian tanks had in fact breached the bypass, crossing Dinpur, Muslim Town and reaching the outskirts of Shankargarh in our heartland. We frantically scrambled our unit together and made a charge for Shankargarh. (**Col. Jaswal** *is now clearly awakened to a familiar theatre of war and barely blinks as he listens.* **Fatima** *sits pensively with her forehead in her hand, looking at the floor)* After three hours of intense fighting over some five square miles, I received a radio message that the 17 Poona Horse have the better of us and that one, or maybe two of their... erm, *your* tanks had destroyed five of our Pattons and are well beyond our lines. I made a solo dart to the spot, with instructions to retreat if deemed fit. Of course, no honourable officer would take that instruction seriously, as you would agree. After about half an hour of seeing nothing untoward, in the distance, I caught a glimpse of an Indian Centurian tank that seemed to be isolated. Drawing closer, I could see that it was already quite badly damaged, probably from shelling it had taken *en route*. We advanced towards one another, two lone rangers in no man's land. At that point of no return, which you instinctively know - and you yourself will well know from all your years in service, Sir – we had to go for it. We fired simultaneously, and it was destiny that I struck the target and he missed.

Both, the Indian tank and the officer were *(swallowing his words)* done for.

Pause.

Sir, that tank was *(Choking)* driven by Lieutenant Mohit.

They all stare into nothingness, with a heavy silence that lingers in flickering candle-light.

Colonel, I don't know if as one soldier to another, it would be in order for me to ask for forgiveness. But I do know one thing. Your son was a true warrior. He fought beyond the call of duty, and it is my honour to be able to tell you today, in person, of how much I admire and respect him.

Brig. Siddiqui *now seems spent, but relieved.* ***Fatima*** *is fighting back tears. Long pause.* ***Col. Jaswal*** *stands up slowly, but steadily, walks to the cabinet near the wall, rests his arm on it. In a near visceral tone, with each word strong and spoken into space.*

Colonel Burgess returned to England after Quetta and we stayed in touch after Independence. I would write to him at his Yorkshire home every Christmas, and he would promptly reply in the new year, with greetings and updates on his family and career. I told him of Mohit's birth in 1950 and he told of his second son's, that very year. Andrew was his name. When Mohit decided to join the National Defence Academy, Burgess was one of the first people I informed. This time he didn't just reply with a letter, but sent me a little parcel as well. It contained a replica of the Victoria Cross, in gun metal with just two words inscribed below – 'For Valour'. It struck me that Britain's highest gallantry award could be so plain... but so real. When Mohit won his Param Vir Chakra posthumously, I informed Colonel Burgess of it and he was *(his voice cracks)* so proud. *(Pause, as he retrieves his composure)* He was also glad that Mohit's tank Famagusta had been returned to India, restored and was on display at the Armoured Corps Centre in Ahmednagar. *(Pause, as **Col. Jaswal** continues to look into space. Now, with greater firmness)* I'm told there is a mess named after Burgess at the Staff College. I plan to visit it when I reach Quetta the day after tomorrow. It will make Mohit happy.

(Pause. Then, with politeness to the Siddiquis) So long then. *(He nods at the couple, and turns to leave. They rise to escort him, in a trance-like state)*

Brig. Siddiqui Khudahafiz, Sir. May God be with you.

Col. Jaswal *(Walks a few steps out of the door. He turns around and says to Fatima)* Ma'am, I'm sorry to have not tried your kheer.

Fatima *(Softly)* Khudahafiz, Bhaijaan.

She is holding her husband's arm, as they stand at the door in semi-darkness. After a few moments, the Colonel turns around and exits. Strains of 'Nit Khair Mangan' play in the background, and slowly get louder. Stage fades to black as the image of the cross-shaped medallion flickers on the screen.

Blackout

Inspired by the life of 2nd Lt. Arun Khetarpal, PVC This is a work of fiction.

British Telecom

Set in 1987 Bangalore, this one-act play switches between Molly's Anglo-Indian home and *Riverside*, which is Peter and Srini's video-cassette library close by. Peter and Srini are an interracial gay couple living in a hostile neighbourhood, who find an affinity with Molly and her 13-year-old nephew, Gogo. Before one knows it, things take an ugly turn revealing the underbelly of societal prejudice against the couple.

British Telecom

(A Play in One Act)

Cast (in order)

The Mascot
Molly *f*, early 50s, Anglo-Indian
Gogo *m*, 13, Molly's nephew
Peter *m*, late 40s, British
Srini *m*, late 40s, Indian
A Policeman

Note to director:

1) *Molly's room and Riverside can be two halves of the stage, separately lit.*
2) *The Mascot is to be clownish in appearance, even grotesque.*

———

The Mascot comes on stage, reciting the following names, slowly but with dramatic effect:

Janet Aalfs. American. Martial artist, poet.

Saara Aalto. Finnish. Singer.

Anne Aasheim. Norwegian. Journalist, editor.

Louise Abbema. French. Painter.

Reza Abdoh. Iranian-American. Theatre director, playwright.

Sir Francis Bacon. English. Philosopher & jurist.

Yetide Badaki. Nigerian. Actor.

Susanne Baer. German. Justice of the Federal Court.

Bai Ling. Chinese American. Actor.

Cristobal Balenciaga. Spanish. Fashion Designer.

Jorge Caballero. Mexican. Actor.

Julius Caesar. Roman. General.

Ece Ayhan Caglar. Turkish. Poet.

Francesco Calcagno. Italian. Friar.

Oliver Callan. Irish. Comedian.

Exits

Scene 1

Bangalore, 1987. Molly's living room. Rosewood cane sofa, a piano, coffee table, few books and photo frames on the what-not, a cross on the wall. Molly, in a chequered dress, is seated at the piano playing a mellow but cheerful piece. She is a greying, elegant woman, with the strength of someone who's seen more than they needed to. Gogo, chubby and bashful, dressed in tight fitted shorts and a T-shirt, is sitting on the floor watching a film on the VCR with an old-school remote in hand.

Gogo: *Grumbling to himself* I hate these songs.

Molly: What did you say?

Gogo: I hate these songs! Why do Hindi films have so many songs?!

Molly: So you can go to the toilet or fix a cup of tea while the actors dance around town.

Gogo: I just FF them.

Molly: FF?

Gogo: Fast forward.

Molly: Which is why that remote is like a sixth finger on your hand!

Gogo: *Grins blankly* Aunt Molly, we should go get some cassettes from Riverside.

Molly: We should, Gogo. Maybe later this evening, if my knitting is done by then.

Gogo: Your knitting never gets done.

Molly: Sonny, that's as your uncle would say. But it gets done you know…… at least in my head. Before which I'm onto knitting something else. Maybe I'm superstitious and never stop…

Gogo: Miss Rose says one should never be superstitious.

Molly: Who is Miss Rose?

Gogo: My new class teacher in 8A… *Hesitates* She's pretty.

Molly: Really? Now, now!

Gogo: *Blushes* And she rides to school on a motorcycle!

Molly: Now that's a first!

Gogo: Yes! All the boys look at her from the assembly when she rides in to school. And the Principal has to raise his voice to get our attention back.

Molly laughs out loud.

Beat. Going towards him and siting on her haunches to speak to him affectionately.

You're growing up so quickly Gogo. I still remember the time you'd look away if a girl was anywhere in the vicinity.

Gogo: I still hate girls.

Molly: And what is your Miss Rose then?

Gogo: She's different.

Molly: She's *different*. How different?! *Molly roughs up his hair. He folds to the floor in faux pain.*

Come along now sonny boy. *She walks smartly towards stage exit.* I'm going to run you a nice hot bath, after which you can have your supper. And we can then go down to Riverside.

Scene 2

Later that evening. A video cassette library on the ground floor of a cosy home called 'Riverside' that belongs to Peter and Srini. Molly and Gogo are browsing the collection, neatly labelled and arranged on wooden shelves. Soft jazz plays in the background on Peter's tape recorder. Peter is standing around, smoking a cigarette. He is white, well built, clean shaven, with an unkempt mop of hair. Wears a loose Hawaiian shirt and khaki trousers. Srini - slim, stubbled, dressed in a kurta and corduroys - sits at a desk with a large register, writing names of films on labels with a sketch pen. He is, in contrast to Peter's gregariousness, introverted to a fault.

Molly: Peter, what is this man! You've had no new tapes for a month now. *She smiles at Srini who waves her a familiar hello.*

Peter: *Putting his cigarette out, in a clipped English accent, which is slightly effeminate* I'm so sorry love! These things come to us from Madras on shipment from Dubai and the two of us have no control over those bullying sheikhs.

Srini smiles at them, looking up from his desk

Molly: Gogo here has been desperate for Top Gun. Anything you can do to help?

Peter: It's on our next consignment in fact. Here, can I tempt him with this instead? *Hands Molly the tape of Rambo III*

Molly: *To Gogo* You want to watch this *bachcha*?

Gogo: *Uninterested* I've watched this twice already

Peter laughs

Molly: Where on earth? Not at that Prithvi's home I hope. *To Peter, softly, as if in private* The boy's two years older than Gogo and gets (*points to a blue mug lying nearby*) these coloured films I hear. Not from you I hope!

Peter: Good heavens, no! *In an even more pronounced English accent* We're connoisseurs of the finest collection of art and popular cinema. A collection Her Majesty would be proud of.

Molly: Then why are you *here* and not catering to the Queen?

Srini laughs quietly.

Peter: My exodus from the homeland is a story best saved for later, Molly. Perhaps over a cup of tea at yours.

Molly: *Nods* Let's do that soon.

Gogo: *Cranky* Can we leave now Aunt Molly? Giant Robot is on the TV in ten minutes.

Molly: Let's rush home then Gogo. Can't have you miss your Thursday evening ritual. See you chaps soon!

Peter: Be well, Molly!

Peter turns the music up, re-lights his cigarette and starts arranging some tapes. Srini returns to his labelling. A Policeman - rugged, aggressive with a protruding belly, an overgrown moustache and bloodshot eyes - walks in, and looks menacingly at Peter and Srini, who are on their feet.

Peter: *Nervously* How may we help you officer?

Policeman: You have Kannada pictures?

Peter: *Slightly relieved, but still on edge* I'm afraid not, officer. But we do have a shelf with Hindi films here if you'd like to browse?

Policeman: *Offended* Hindi is not Kannada, Saar. I want Kannada.

Peter: My profuse apologies, we'll try and get some Kanarese films soon.

Policeman: Snaps Kannada Saar, not Canarese! At least that much you can learn after coming here no?

Peter: *Shaking* Kannada, Kannada, I'm so sorry! I'm just a little nervous.

Policeman: Why nervous Saar? You have done anything illegal?

Peter: No, of course not!

Srini: Sir, we are just running this library for the locality... Lot of neighbours from the area come and borrow tapes. The Commissioner also comes sometimes.

Policeman: Police commissioner comes here?

Srini: Yes sir, he lives nearby.

Policeman: *Slightly guarded now* Oh. Ok. I did know that.

Peter: Could we show you some new tapes officer?

Policeman waves him off, and browses a little before beginning to leave. Stops at the door, turns around and glares at the two men who are visibly scared.

Scene 3

Molly's living room, later that evening. She sits in a comfortable chair, while concentrating on the crossword in the newspaper with a thick pair of glasses on the tip of her nose and a pen in her hand.

Molly: *Reading the cryptic clue aloud* 'Gives you headrush, could have tea and all'. Five letters……

Gogo: *Sad* Aunt Molly, Peter and Srini are so sweet, aren't they?

Molly looks up from her crossword.

Molly: Yes, they are my dear. You seem a little upset…

Gogo: I don't like it when the boys in the locality say such mean things about them.

Molly: *Slightly agitated* Like what? Who does?

Gogo: The boys I play football with. They say they are eunuchs and call them 'pansy', 'fags'…

Molly: And what do you do then Gogo?

Gogo: I just look away. And then they tease me. They say I want to grow up to be like Peter and Srini…

Molly stands, worked up, throwing the newspaper on the table,.

Molly: Oh, these little rascals! I'll pull their tongues out one day, you just see.

Gogo: Just leave it, Aunt Molly. I'm telling you this as a secret.

Molly: Yes, yes son. It's our secret. But don't take it to heart, OK? *Hugs him.*

Gogo: *Hesitates* You know Aunt Molly, the other day I went to return the cassettes, I saw Srini playing with Peter's hair...

Molly: Well that's perfectly normal Gogo... maybe not normal here... but it's quite normal... abroad.

Gogo: Is it?

Molly: Yes. When I was in London with your late uncle Sam in the 1970s, I worked at British Telecom as an operator. I'd often connect lovers to one another and even convey their messages across. Once, an American man, Gerald asked me to propose marriage to his English lover, John.

Gogo: What! Is that allowed?

Molly: I'm not sure, but what the hell, you can't shoot the messenger!

Gogo: So, did John say yes?

Molly: Yes!

Gogo: And did they... erm, get married?

Molly: I wouldn't know Gogo... but I still remember John's voice quaking as he accepted. *She gushes in reminiscence*

Gogo: That's so lovely Aunt Molly. Do we permit such marriages in India?

Molly: No sonny boy, we penalize them.

Gogo: We... pe-na-li-ze them?

Molly: We punish them Gogo. There, you've learnt a new word today.

Gogo: But why do we punish them? I mean... who is being bothered by two people getting married if they want to?

Molly: I wish I could answer that easily Gogo.

Gogo: It doesn't make sense.

Molly: No it doesn't, son.

Gogo: But can't we do something about this?

Molly: *Mildly exasperated* We? As in you and me? I doubt that. If you grow up to become a politician or a lawyer, maybe *you* can do something about it.

Gogo: *Squirms* Politician, never!

Molly: *Laughs* They're not all bad you know... Ok, a lawyer maybe?

Gogo: *Thinking* A lawyer... may be. *Now excited* Like my nana!

Molly: Yes, and a fine lawyer he was. Always available to those who needed him.

Gogo: I miss him so much.

Molly: I do too, sonny boy. But remember, he smiles down upon you from up there.

Gogo looks to the ceiling, straining his neck, and smiles.

Such a handsome man, your grandfather was. *Looking at a black & white photograph in a frame.* Wore a tie even when dining at home.

Gogo: He taught me how to tie a knot on his necktie... but I've now forgotten how.

Molly: I'll show you how someday Gogo. I used to tie one for him often.

Scene 4

Riverside. A few days later.

Peter: Hello there Gogs! Come on in.

Gogo: Hello Uncle Peter, just wanted to return Irma La Douce.

Peter: Your Aunt Molly loves this film, doesn't she? She's borrowed it thrice at least.

Gogo: Yes, she says it reminds her of her trip to Paris with Uncle Sam in... 1972... I think.

Peter: Oh, Paris! Heaven on earth...

Gogo: I really want to go sometime. *Excitedly* We've applied for a passport for me you know Uncle Peter?

Peter: Ah! Good luck lad. It'll come through.

Gogo: Thank you. In a few weeks they say. *Pause.* I should be off.

Peter: Don't you want to borrow a tape?

Gogo: I can't. *Stoically* I have my mid-term exams starting on Monday and Aunt Molly has sealed the VCR. *Srini laughs softly from his desk.*

Turning to leave See you later then, Uncle Peter.

Peter: See you soon Gogo!

Scene 5

Molly's living room, some days later. Late afternoon. A pot of tea with cups, fruit cake and biscuits on the coffee-table.

Peter: Excellent tea, love! Very little milk, just like we like it back home.

Molly: I'm sorry there aren't any scones to keep you company.

Peter: Or clotted cream. They say of the few things the English have gotten right, afternoon tea is one.

Molly: And theatre. *Wistfully* How I miss West End... Wyndham's and The Pinter.

Peter: Ah, bliss...

Molly: Srini, won't you have some more tea? *Srini smiles and nods like he's had enough.* Tell me Peter, why do you call your home Riverside?

Peter: Nothing too complicated there Molly. I grew up by the river Sowe in Coventry and this is, well, tribute.

Molly: Didn't Srini have a say in this?

Srini: *Softly* I like that name too. Coventry is where Peter and I met.

Molly: Oh that's nice!

Gogo: *From stage side, sitting on a floor cushion with a comic book in hand* What did you do there Uncle Peter?

Peter: I worked with the local town council as an employee manager.

Molly: And what took you there Srini?

Peter: *Volunteering* He was up there for a course in automotive design. We met at the council office when he came in for a part-time job.

Molly: And the rest is history.

They laugh.

Peter: And you Molly. Why did you leave the UK?

Molly: *Steely* Gogo's uncle Sam passed away quite suddenly and my folks wanted me back. They felt an Indian woman would struggle to get by herself in a foreign land. *Bitterly* How I wish I had defied them.

Peter: We're sorry to hear that Molly. It couldn't have been easy.

Molly: It wasn't. What with Gogo's mum passing away within a few years of my returning home. There were seven of us, and our Tibetan Lhasa 'Skipper', who lived in this house at one time. Now, it's just the two of us...

Beat.

You know gentlemen, Gogo's mother was a stunner. She passed on a few months before you moved to the neighbourhood. All of 44 and fighting fit. One morning, she fell in the bathroom. And we could do nothing. And this young man here *(pointing to Gogo)* was awfully brave about it. He locked himself in the room when he heard the news. We were petrified. But he emerged in a few minutes, fully composed, with a letter in hand that he kept on his mother's chest as she lay in the coffin... I never read that note. And *(with apparent pride)* Gogo's never looked back since.

I could've never have gone back after. I used to tell Sandy, my sister, how I'd return to England one day. To the charm of Basingstoke and the hour long train ride to Waterloo, which I took six days a week while divided time in London.

But here we are.

And there are no complaints.

Peter: You are a strong woman Molly. An exemplar. *Trying to easy up the conversation* What sun-sign are you?

Molly bursts out laughing.

Molly: Like those things matter Peter! I'm Aquarian, since you ask.

Peter: Really? So am I! The January side of Aquarian, if I may probe?

Molly: Indeed. The 28th.

Peter: No way! I'm 28th January too... Good Lord! And what sign are you Gogo?

Gogo: Cancerian.

Peter: Wait. What? No! So is Srini! Tell me now, not the...

Gogo: The 18th.

Peter: Good. Blooming. Hell. So is Srini! This cannot be mere coincidence. *As if in a trance, looking at Srini who has his eyes wide open in wonderment* This is bizarre...

Molly: Jesus, it sure is! *Sternly.* You're not cooking this up are you Peter?

Peter: Of course not Molly. I could show you our passports.

Molly: That true Srini? You seem more reliable.

Srini nods with a big smile.

Gogo: Wow, this really is amazing Aunt Molly!

Molly: It is, sonny boy. I've never ever met someone who shares *even* my birthday.

Peter: This is surreal. I feel dizzy......

Molly: This calls for a combined birthday celebration next week, Peter!

Peter: *Tou-ché!*

Molly: 4 pm at mine on the 28th? And I'm not calling to remind.

Peter: We shall be at your door at 4 pm, Molly. *Stands up to leave.*

Molly: Good! I'll make Vindaloo.

Scene 6

Riverside. Later that evening. Srini at his desk, filling in labels. Peter is pasting them on new video cassettes.

Peter: Lovely afternoon at Molly's today.

Srini nods with a smile.

She really is quite vivacious. And those years in England served her well. *Winks.*

Beat.

We'll be alright Srini?

Srini looks up from his desk.

Will we be... alright?

I mean, is there a future here... is it even *safe*? Shouldn't we be moving back to Coventry... before the end of this year. *Srini does not respond.*

Or early next year even?

Pleading. I know you have commitments here Srini, but this is no place for people like us. You know?

Srini looks at him blankly. Peter pulls up a chair and sits in front of the desk, and holds Srini's hands in his.

I just have a bad feeling. That's all. It should pass...

Long silence.

Srini sings, softly, in Afro-American Gospel style, in a voice quite different from his usual reticent self:

> *There aint no bird*
> *In them autumn sky;*
> *No cloud in sight*
> *To mine naked eye.*
>
> *No rain that falls*
> *On them thirsty stones.*
> *No warm bed waits*
> *For them tired bones.*
>
> *But I have you*
> *Mine sweetest love.*
> *Mine sweetest love...*
> *I have you.*

Scene 7

Molly's living room. Some balloons on the windows. Molly is dressed brightly and busily arranges her table. Gogo helps bring goodies from the kitchen. The Mascot sits at a chair by the window, drink in hand, invisible to the others. Happy music plays in the background as the doorbell rings.

Peter: *Offstage* It's us!

Molly: There in a moment. Gogo, go get the door. Quick!

Peter: Happy birthday my love! *Kisses her cheeks in elaborate ceremony.*

Molly: Thank you my dear! And happy birthday to *you*!

Srini kisses both her cheeks, and pats Gogo on his.

Peter: A little something from Riverside for you Molly. *Hands her a ribboned present.* And we shan't ask how old you are today!

Molly: *Eagerly opening the box.* Oh I can't wait to see what it is! Cannot remember the last time someone gave me a gift... *Looking mischievously at Gogo.*

Gogo: But I gave you a rose from our garden, didn't I?

Molly: *Kanjoos!*

Peter and Srini laugh.

Molly: *Ripping open the present* Gosh, it's lovely... a coffee table book on the Kew Gardens. I love it gentlemen!

Peter: *Bows in courtesy.*

Srini: *Softly* I picked it... from our library.

Molly: Oh Srini... there's something nice and warm in receiving a book from someone's library. Like art from someone's walls. It's a piece of them you possess. Thank you. *Hands it to Gogo to keep it on her coffee table. He eyes it briefly before laying it down.*

Molly: Now come help yourself, before we sit down. *As if reading from a menu.* There's vindaloo and bread, scotched eggs, *kheema* samosas and marble cake. And some mulled wine. Not leftovers from Christmas I can promise.

Peter: That would be fine, Molly. Wine ages well, just as you have. *Twinkle in his eye.*

Molly: Oh you're such a charmer, Peter! Now fill your plates, will you?

Peter: Absolutely! Come on, Srini, let's eat up. *To Molly* But the cake will be birthday cake, I hope.

Gogo: Yes! It's chocolate, with fifty six candles.

Molly: Don't you give away my age now, young man!

Music. They get drunk. Mascot does too. Laughing, singing and some dancing on stage, as the background music gets louder. Molly and Peter can be heard singing lines from 'Sweet Caroline' and 'Swing Low, Sweet Chariot'. The Mascot ad libs the words to himself.

Molly: *As the music slowly fades...* Time for us to have our cake and eat it too... go on Gogo, light those candles. And add one for Peter too!

Gogo lights candles with the numbers '5' and '6', and one single candle, as Molly and Peter cut the cake together and the others sing 'Happy Birthday'. (Mascot sings along, rising from his chair.)

Peter: *Picking up his glass* A toast to the most beautiful and vivacious woman in all of South India! *The others clink their glasses, Gogo with a bottle of ThumsUp. Mascot raises a glass from his corner.*

Srini: *Stands up, gingerly* I'm really not one for speeches, as you'd have easily guessed. But I do still want to say something today. Molly, first things first, happy birthday. And many happy returns. And, of course, happy birthday Peter. I just want to say that I'm... happy... here, at last. I've found love and happiness maybe for the first time in my life......

Now drawing on painful nostalgia Growing up in Rameswaram, all I got were taunts and abuses.

Some physical abuse too that I'll avoid on this special occasion. College in Guindy was no better and then... I got married. *Molly's eyes widen.* Yes, for a few years to a nice Tamilian girl before we called it quits. For obvious reasons. My father was a Gandhian and was stoutly opposed to dowry. We had to return the single silver coin Lakshmi's family gave us... Lakshmi was my wife. Her brothers wanted to file a criminal case against us but luckily a Dr Abdul Kalam - who is from our town - mediated the dispute. He was known to my father from their college days in Rameswaram. He's now a big scientist in Delhi or somewhere. And would you believe it, I (*looking for the right phrase, conscious of Gogo's presence*) had never "done it" even when I divorced... (*looks sheepishly at Molly*) I'm sorry if I'm rambling but I just wanted to say... it's only after all this nonsense... this trauma, that I moved to Coventry on work and met Peter and am now... somewhat happy......

Peter: // Somewhat?!

Srini: //... that I'm *very* happy.

With pain in his voice And I feel like you understand me Molly. You *and* Gogo. So thank you for your friendship. *Sits.*

Molly: *Visibly moved, despite her strong demeanour* Awww, what a lovely speech Srini. And I've never heard you talk so much in all these years! It must be the wine. Let me say how fond I am of both you boys. All three of you actually! *Ruffles Gogo's hair*. It's a strange affinity we have...

Maybe because of my days in the UK or... maybe because you two have been the least judgemental since my return. When Sam died in Basingstoke of a damaged liver, I returned to India as a widow and had people avoid me at the grocery store, look away when we crossed each other at the park and (*angrily*) even have the audacity to come to my dad to ask him to get me married again. Because that was how "our society works". To keep Dad happy I even once went on a date to size up a suitor - a widower himself who ran a business in Colombo. We met at the Windsor Manor and I made sure I ordered the most expensive wine on the menu. A few drinks down I was quite giggly and told him he reminded me of my brother. (*Cheekily*) By the way, I have none... I can still remember his face lose colour as he paid the bill and walked me to an autorickshaw. He didn't even drop me home! (*Laughs*) Dad was very amused with this story as he never really, in his heart, wanted to force me to get married again. Twenty years later, here we are on my birthday. So... cheers to life!

All: Cheers!

Beat.

Molly: Coming back to what we were saying, I think it's also a Bangalore thing, you know Peter? The city has more of a cosmopolitan feel, more people who've lived and worked abroad... they have a better world view, wouldn't you say.

Peter: *Sarcastically* Most definitely. Like those boys who come to our window every other night shouting 'Ho-mos! Ho-mos!'

Molly: *Enraged* Gogo, is this your gang doing this nonsense!?

Gogo: *In exasperation* They're not MY gang!

Molly: *Realising she's upset him* I know, I know son. But I'll have their hide one day, you just see! What schools do they go to?!

Peter: Let this be now love... Maybe I'm judging Bangalore too harshly based on a few imbeciles. But Srini and I have talked often about going back to Coventry... Haven't we Srini?

Srini: *Nods, silently* Must we bring this up now? You know I'd move if we could... I need some time...

Lights fade on all except Gogo, who moves upstage

Gogo: I don't know what problem these boys in the locality have with Peter and Srini. They taunt and joke about them in such a bad way... it hurts. But they're like that with everyone actually. When Kanna's sister was coming home on the Luna, they laughed and whistled at her. Poor Kanna - he was standing right there and couldn't do anything. And that Bugsy - he was mocking

Kanna 'What man, cat got your tongue? You'll go running home to your mummy now or what!' And they all laughed. I wanted to say something, to tell them not to talk to Kanna like this but I kept quiet. Otherwise, they would turn on me. I'm younger than them and not very fast in football. (Blushing) need to lose some weight. But... the boys don't gang up on me that much. I think they're little scared of Aunt Molly. And I also bring them new footballs whenever needed. I meaning, Aunt Molly buys them for me and I take them to the gang. So they let me be mostly. I don't tell anyone they smoke behind the slide also...... Why can't these boys just be... *Searching*... decent?

Riverside, soon after. Dim lights on an empty room. Loud voices of young boys off-stage.

'Ho-mos! Ho-mos! Ho-mos!'

Peter rushes onstage, towards the window

'Oh get lost you buggers! Get lost!'.

The boys can be heard laughing loudly as they disperse. Peter crumples onto the sofa, head in hand.

Scene 8

Riverside. A few days later. Night. The doorbell rings. And rings again, repeatedly. Peter comes rushing onstage, hurriedly buttoning his shirt, and answers the door to find the Policeman outside

Policeman: *To Peter, reading from a document* Mr Peter... Ian Botham?

Peter: Peter *Higginbotham*, yes.

Policeman: Come with me Saar.

Peter: Come where?

Policeman: Come Saar. *Firmly* There is a case.

Peter: What case officer? What have I done?

Policeman: *Indignant* What have you done!? You come here on a tourist visa and run this video business and all.

Peter: Oh no, this is a labour of love!

Policeman: *Mocking him* Labour? You do some *coolie* work here?

Peter: Uh... no... also, this business is in my partner's name.

Policeman: So he is your partner?

Peter: Yes. I mean no! Not like a business partner.

Policeman: Then like what partner Saar?

Peter: Like... like, a friend.

Policeman: Saar, don't come here and spoil our culture. And our childrens. *Now impatient* Come, come!

Srini: *Helpless* Sir, please wait...

Policeman: Who are you!?

Srini: Srini.

Policeman: Full name saar!

Srini: Err... Srini... Srinivasan Paramasivan

Policeman: You are also on visa?

Srini: No, I'm Indian.

Policeman: Good. Be Indian then.

Peter leaves with the policeman, bewildered. Srini leans on the table, ashen.

Scene 9

A prison cell. Peter sits alone on a stone bed, haggard, head in hands. Long silence.

The Mascot comes on stage and sings the song from Scene 5, in a deeper, more poignant tone.

There aint no bird
In them autumn sky;
No cloud in sight
To mine naked eye.

No rain that falls
On them thirsty stones.
No warm bed waits
For them tired bones.

But I have you
Mine sweetest love.
Mine sweetest love...
I have you.

Scene 10

The prison cell. Peter kneels at his bed, shakily reciting the Lord's Prayer, while the Mascot watches him from stage corner:

Our Father,
who art in heaven,
hallowed be thy name......

The Mascot, mocking him, and speaking over him:

Our Peter
who art far from heaven,
callow be thy name;
they redemption come
thy will be finally done
on earth
but surely not in heaven.

Give him this day his daily bread
and charge him for his trespasses

More agitated now

as we charge those
who trespass against us;

and lead us into *our* redemption
and deliver us from evil.

Amen.

Peter looks at him plaintively.

Scene 11

Molly's. Few days later.

Molly: *Visibly upset* Did you hear about Peter?

Gogo: Yes. That he was arrested for fraud or something.

Molly: What fraud?! He ran a poor little video library that gave this wretched locality some joy.

Gogo: But the boys were saying it was some financial thing. Smuggling or something like that...

Molly: Nonsense! The neighbours complained against them for living together as two men and the cops cooked up some case to send him back to England.

Gogo: *In desperation* Is it an offence for two men to even live together Aunt Molly?

Molly: It seems it is, Gogo. Some section in the penal code I heard.... (*Pained*) Loving someone can be an offence now.

Gogo: That's not fair.

Molly: It is not, sonny boy. It is not. (*Almost choked*) And you remember this. When you grow up, love whomsoever you choose. Whomsoever.

Gogo: *After a pause* Even if it is illegal?

Molly: *With a sense of bravado* Things will change. Just you watch. You know Gogo, it was an offence in England too. And then so many important people, like Ian McKellen and Michael Cashman campaigned against it that their parliament had to change the law. After four hundred bloody years. And *their* law, an Englishman's outdated law, is now applied in India to arrest an Englishman. Absurd!

Gogo: Ian McK......? *Beat.* Uncle Peter was such a friendly person. *Almost crying now.* And he shares his birthday with you.

Molly: *Hugging him* As Srini does with you, Gogo... We should go see him sometime. He's always so quiet...... poor Srini.

Molly goes to her piano, plays a slow, melancholic piece. Lights fade on Molly's living room, as the music continues. The lights dimly light up Riverside, where the figure of Srini can be seen stroking Peter's hair.

The Mascot comes to stage front, reciting more names:

Yona Wallach. Israeli. Poet.
Sarah Waters. Welsh. Novelist.
Tennessee Williams. American. Playwright.
Oscar Wilde. Irish. Playwright.
Virginia Woolf. English. Actor.

The actors join in, one by one, in chorus:

Marta Xargay. Spanish. Basketball player.
Xian. Chinese. LGBTQ activist.
Olive Yang. Burmese. Drug trafficker.
Jwan Yosef. Syrian-Swedish. Artist.
Hamid Zaher. Afghan. Writer.
Peter Higginbotham. English. Video library owner.
Srini Paramasivan. Indian. Video library owner.

Blackout

www.ingramcontent.com/pod-product-compliance
Lightning Source LLC
Chambersburg PA
CBHW020505160726
47991CB00007B/2816